No-Bake
Gingerbread
Houses
FOR KIDS

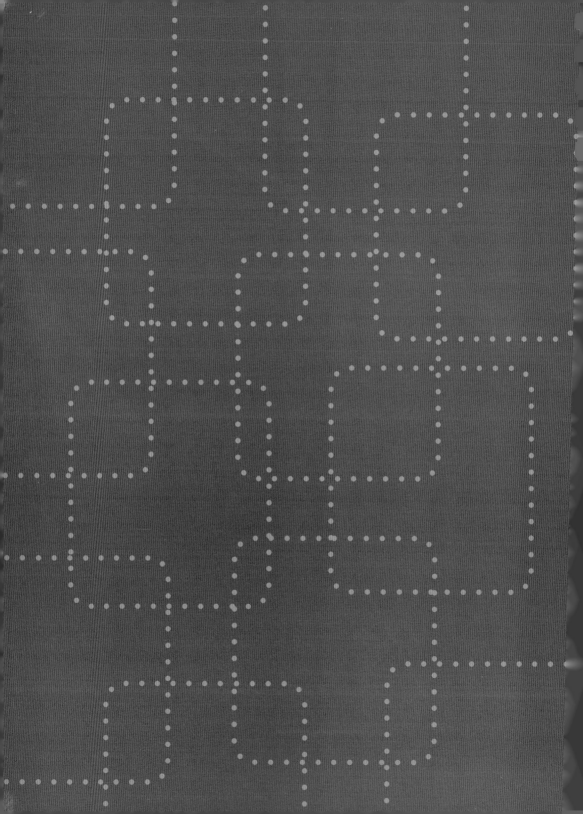

No-Bake
Gingerbread
Houses
FOR KIDS

LISA TURNER ANDERSON

Photographs by Zac Williams

GIBBS SMITH
TO ENRICH AND INSPIRE HUMANKIND

for Matt and Malcolm

First Edition
14 13 12 11 10   6 5 4 3 2

Text © 2010 Lisa Turner Anderson
Photographs © 2010 Zac Williams

Published by
Gibbs Smith
P.O. Box 667
Layton, Utah 84041

1.800.835.4993 orders
www.gibbs-smith.com

Designed by Dawn DeVries Sokol
Manufactured in Shenzhen, China in July, 2010 by Toppan Printing Co.
Gibbs Smith books are printed on either recycled, 100% post-consumer waste, FSC-certified papers or on paper produced from a 100% certified sustainable forest/controlled wood source.

Library of Congress Cataloging-in-Publication Data

Anderson, Lisa Turner.
  No-bake gingerbread houses for kids / Lisa Turner Anderson ; photographs by Zac Williams. — 1st ed.
     p. cm.
  ISBN-13: 978-1-4236-0590-4
  ISBN-10: 1-4236-0590-X
  1. Gingerbread houses. 2. Cookery (Cold dishes) I. Title.
  TX771.A58 2010
  745.5—dc22
                    2010003541

CONTENTS

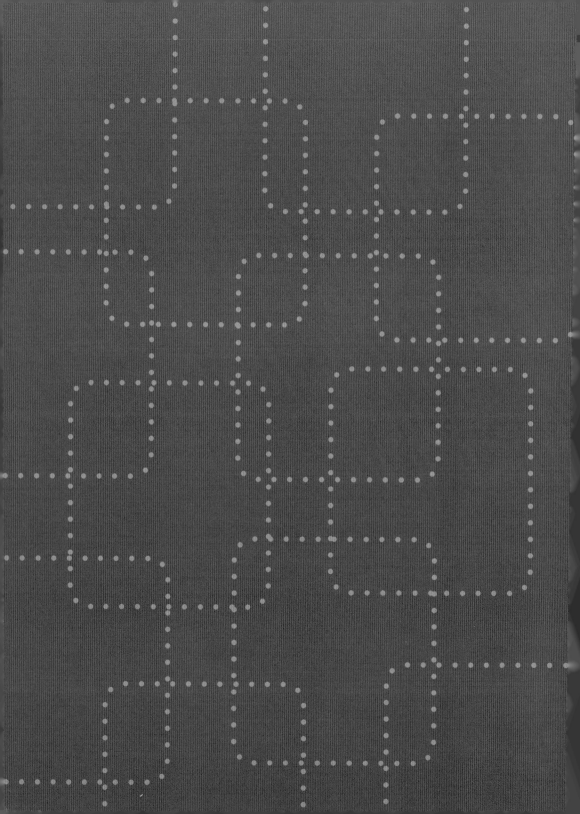

GETTING STARTED

Making no-bake gingerbread houses is easy, fun, and best of all, fast! This book will show you how to make houses, castles, cottages, and more using graham crackers, cookies, ice cream cones, waffle bowls, and candy. There's no need to mix dough, roll it out, bake it, and wait for it to harden. The house structures in this book take only minutes to make, meaning you can get to the decorating more quickly—and that's the best part. Before you begin, you just need to know a few tips. Then you'll be on your way to having fun!

Where to Build the House

A large piece of cardboard—at least 1 foot by 1 foot—is the best base to build your house on. It's sturdy enough to pick up so that you can move your house easily. Be sure to cover your cardboard with waxed paper or aluminum foil so the frosting doesn't seep through.

Even if the house is small and doesn't take up much room on the cardboard, you'll still want a large base so that you have plenty of room for decorating. The instructions for most of the houses in this book suggest that you spread icing around the house, such as green for grass or white for snow. Covering the whole cardboard base with icing helps your house look nice and neat.

Graham Crackers

While not all the houses in this book are made with graham crackers, most of them are. Building structures out of graham crackers requires a few tricks.

Most houses in the book require that you cut graham crackers into shapes or smaller pieces. Instead of trying to break them with your hands, have an adult use a serrated knife, such as a steak knife, to gently saw the cracker along the lines until the unwanted piece breaks off. If you try to break them with your hands, the pieces will usually break off unevenly.

The diagrams for each house will show you the sizes and shapes of the graham crackers you need. The blue parts of the diagram are the pieces of the crackers that need to be cut off and thrown away.

For many of the houses, you will need to "glue" two or more graham crackers together with icing to make a larger front, side, back, or roof piece. To help the pieces stay together, you will need to "glue" a quarter graham cracker across the seam, as shown in Diagram 1. This will help you make larger and more interesting houses without worrying about them falling apart. When you put the house together, make sure the quarter crackers are on the inside of the house.

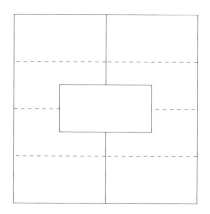

Diagram 1

Royal Icing

Making gingerbread houses requires special icing called royal icing. It is made with egg whites, water, and powdered sugar, and it is very strong, like glue. It dries to a hard candy-like finish that will last for months. You can use either raw egg whites or meringue powder (which has dried egg whites) to make the icing. While both versions make equally strong icing, I prefer using meringue powder because it's easier to use and safer to eat than raw egg whites. You can find meringue powder at craft or cake decorating stores.

Egg White Royal Icing

3 egg whites
$1/2$ teaspoon cream of tartar
4 cups powdered sugar

Beat the egg whites and cream of tartar together until the meringue has formed stiff peaks (meaning when you lift the beaters out of the meringue, it stands up straight and doesn't fall over). Beat in the powdered sugar, 1 cup at a time, until mixed together and smooth.

Meringue Powder Royal Icing

$1/4$ cup meringue powder
$1/2$ cup water
4 cups powdered sugar

Beat the meringue powder and water together until the meringue has formed stiff peaks (meaning when you lift the beaters out of the meringue, it stands up straight and doesn't fall over). Beat in the powdered sugar, 1 cup at a time, until mixed together and smooth.

Tinting the icing with food coloring is a fun and easy way to add more color to your houses. Gel food coloring works the best because it is super concentrated and makes deep, bright colors. You can find gel food coloring in most grocery stores, but the gels at craft and cake decorating stores come in many more colors and are even more concentrated.

When tinting your icing, use a craft stick or toothpick to add just a tiny bit of gel to the icing. A little bit goes a very long way. You can always keep adding more, but you can't add less!

The easiest way to use the icing to decorate your house is to spoon some of it into a quart-size ziplock bag. Squeeze the air out of the top, then seal the bag. Double-check and make sure it is completely sealed or else the icing will come out the top when you squeeze the bag. Cut off a bottom corner of the bag and squeeze the bag to push the icing through the hole. The smaller the hole, the thinner the line when you're piping the icing. You'll usually want a thinner line when decorating, but you can use a thicker line when "gluing" the house together.

Any icing that is left in the bowl needs to be covered with plastic wrap so that the plastic wrap is touching the surface of the icing. Icing that is exposed to air will turn hard quickly and you won't be able to use it.

You can store royal icing in the fridge for a few days.

Candy, Candy, Candy!

The projects in this book have suggestions of what candy to use so that your house looks the same as the one in the photo. But if you have an idea for a different color or shape of candy for the house you're making, go for it! The best part of making gingerbread houses is using your imagination and playing with different candies to come up with a cool design that's all your own. You can use any candy you want, with one exception: taffy. After taffy is unwrapped, it will eventually "melt" and run down the sides of your house. Trust me—it doesn't look good!

Now that you know some tips and tricks and important information, go have some fun, be creative, and build some really cool no-bake gingerbread houses.

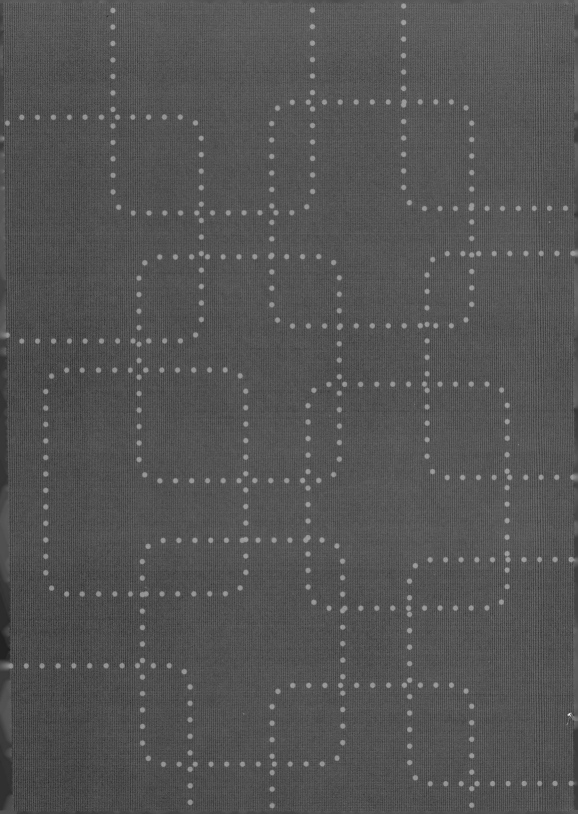

EASY CANDY COTTAGE

Graham crackers
 (see diagrams)
1 batch white royal icing

Decorations
• Sour Skittles
• jelly fruit slices
• candy canes
• peppermints
• gumdrops

1 Using royal icing, "glue" the house together with the vertical point crackers for the front and back and two horizontal whole crackers for the sides.

2 Pipe royal icing along the slanted lines of the point crackers. Glue the two remaining graham crackers on the slanted edges to form the roof. Pipe a line of icing along the top of the roof and gently push the roof pieces together.

3 Decorate as desired.

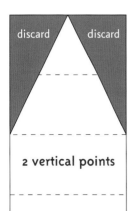

discard   discard

2 vertical points

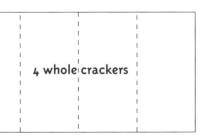

4 whole crackers

LOLLIPOP LANE

Graham crackers
(see diagrams)

1 batch white royal icing

Decorations
- lollipops
- Starbursts
- candy sticks
- jelly beans
- jelly fruit slices

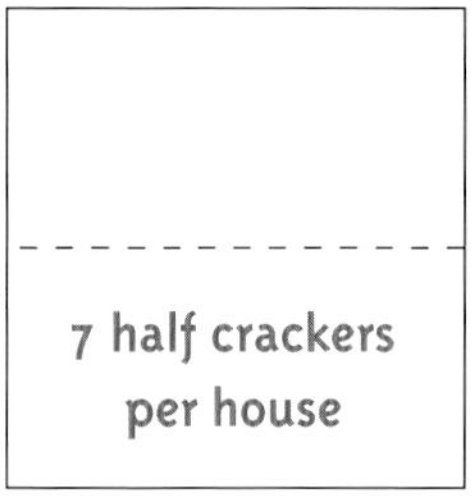

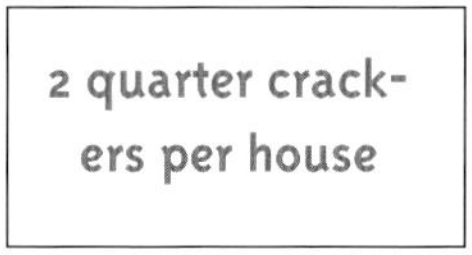

1 Cut a half cracker in half diagonally to make two triangles. Using royal icing, "glue" a triangle to the top of a half cracker. "Glue" a quarter graham cracker across the seam to help the two pieces stick together. Repeat to make a second triangle-topped piece.

2 Make the house using the triangle-topped pieces you just made for the front and back of the house, and a half graham cracker for each side. Pipe icing along the slanted rooflines and place two half crackers on top for the roof.

3 Repeat steps 1 and 2 to make two more houses.

7 half crackers
per house

2 quarter crack-
ers per house

4 Decorate with candy. To make orange bricks, cut orange jelly fruit slices into rectangles. To make the sidewalk squares, flatten purple Starburst candies and lay them in a row. Have an adult use a sharp pair of scissors to cut the candy sticks to the length of the house.

SWEETHEART COTTAGE

Graham crackers
  (see diagrams)

¹/₂ batch white
  royal icing

¹/₂ batch brown
  royal icing

Decorations

- large red hearts
- small red and
  pink hearts

1 To make the front of the house, cut a whole cracker in half diagonally to make two long skinny triangles. Using white icing, "glue" the triangles together along the long straight edges. "Glue" a quarter cracker across the seam. "Glue" this piece to the long edge of one bottom piece. Then "glue" two quarter crackers across the seam.

2 Repeat step 1 to create the back of the house.

3 Put the house together using the front and back pieces and two horizontal whole crackers for the sides. "Glue" two whole crackers on each side for the roof.

4 Cover the front, back, and sides with brown icing. Decorate the front using candy hearts. Cover the roof with white icing. Decorate using candy hearts.

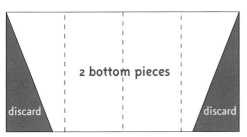

discard   2 bottom pieces   discard

8 whole crackers

6 quarter crackers

FAIRY TREE HOUSE

1 batch pink royal icing

16 (3-inch) molasses
  cookies

2 large flat-bottom
  waffle bowls, such
  as Joy or Kroger

About 40 spearmint
  leaves

Necco wafers

Jelly beans

Decorations
• gumdrops
• sour straws
• chocolate pebbles
• blue decorating
  sugar

1 Using royal icing, "glue" eight molasses cookies together in a stack. Glue a waffle bowl upside down on top of the stack. Repeat with the remaining eight cookies and second waffle bowl to make a second stack, then glue the second stack on top of the first. If the "tree" is leaning, adjust it to make it straight.

2 Cut all the spearmint leaves into two layers. Stick leaves in a row along the bottom edge of one of the waffle bowls. (The leaves should be sticky enough that you won't have to use icing.) Add a second row of spearmint leaves above the first row, staggering them. Keep making rows until the whole waffle bowl is covered. Repeat with the second waffle bowl.

3 Glue Necco wafers to the tree for windows, then make window frames

with icing. Using icing, draw a door at the bottom center of the tree and add a jelly bean doorknob.

4 Make a cobblestone path using speckled jelly beans. Use sour straws cut into small pieces for grass. Use pieces of gumdrops to make mushrooms. Use chocolate pebbles and blue sugar to make the brook.

EASTER BUNNY HOUSE

¹/₃ batch white
   royal icing

¹/₃ batch yellow
   royal icing

¹/₃ batch green
   royal icing

Graham crackers (see
   diagrams next page)

Decorations

• Necco wafers
• jelly beans
• Dum-Dums
• gumdrops
• flower confetti
• chocolate
   sandwich cookies
• candy corn

1 To make the front of the house, use white icing to "glue" two three-quarters crackers together along the longer edges. "Glue" a quarter cracker across the seam to help the two pieces stay together. Repeat to make the back of the house.

2 To make one side of the house, "glue" a quarter cracker to the bottom of a vertical point piece. "Glue" a quarter cracker across the seam to help the two pieces stay together. "Glue" the front, back, and sides together to make the house. "Glue" the remaining three-quarters crackers on top to make the roof.

3 Cover the house with yellow icing. "Glue" Necco wafers to the roof. Make windows using different colors of jelly beans for the windowpanes and white icing for the window frames. Draw a door using white icing and use a jelly bean for the doorknob. Pipe icing in front of the door to create a

6 three-quarters crackers

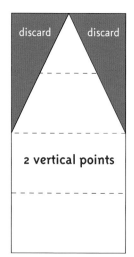

discard   discard

2 vertical points

6 quarter crackers

path, and sprinkle flower confetti on the path. Spread green frosting around the house to make the yard. "Glue" gumdrops, Dum-Dums, and green spearmint leaves around the house to make flowers.

4 To make the carrot garden, crush chocolate sandwich cookies and sprinkle them in a square section of the yard. Cut the yellow and white parts off the candy corn, leaving the orange as the carrot. Make a little dent in the top of each carrot and insert a green piece of flower confetti. Place the carrots in rows in the dirt.

MERMAID PALACE

1/3 batch white
  royal icing

1/3 batch purple
  royal icing

2/3 batch seafoam-
  green royal icing

29 vanilla sandwich
  cookies

3 sugar cones

Smarties

Decorations
- sour gummy
  worms
- gumdrops
- green sour straws
- candy seashells

1 To make the short tower, use white icing to "glue" seven sandwich cookies together in a stack. "Glue" a sugar cone upside down on top. Repeat to make the middle tower, this time using ten sandwich cookies. Repeat again to make the tall tower, this time using twelve sandwich cookies.

2 Cover the tower tops with purple icing and the tower bottoms with seafoam-green icing. Make the windows using Smarties for the windowpanes and purple icing for the window frames.

3 Make sea anemones using sour gummy worms cut in half. Make a sea sponge using upside-down gumdrops. Make seaweed using green sour straws.

COZY CABIN

1 batch white royal icing, with about ½ cup tinted dark yellow

Graham crackers (see diagrams next page)

44 Pepperidge Farm Mint Chocolate Pirouette cookies

Pretzel sticks

Graham sticks

Sugar cones

Decorations
• Spearmint leaves

1 Using royal icing, make one side of the roof by "gluing" three whole crackers together in a row along the long edges. "Glue" a quarter cracker across each seam to help the pieces stay together. Repeat to make the second side of the roof. Set aside the two roof pieces to dry.

2 To make the front of the house, "glue" two three-quarters graham crackers together along the longer sides. "Glue" the long side of a horizontal point piece along the top of the two crackers. "Glue" a quarter cracker across each seam to help all the pieces stay together. Repeat to make the back of the house.

3 Make one side of the house by "gluing" two three-quarters crackers together along the long edges. "Glue" a quarter cracker across the seams. Repeat to make the second side.

6 whole crackers

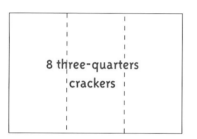

8 three-quarters crackers

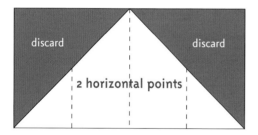

discard   discard

2 horizontal points

12 quarter crackers

4 "Glue" the four sides together to make the house, making sure that the quarter seam crackers are on the inside of the house.

5 "Glue" a Pirouette cookie along the bottom of the house front. One end of the cookie should be even with the left edge of the house and the other end should stick out past the right edge. "Glue" another cookie on top of the first cookie, staggering it so that the end sticks out past the left edge. Keep adding cookies this way on all sides of the house. You will need to cut some of the cookies to fit the top front and top back of the house.

6 Pipe icing along the slanted rooflines and gently place each roof piece on top of the house, making sure the quarter seam crackers are on the inside. Cover the roof with icing and add icicles made of icing to the front eaves.

7 Make the windows and door out of pretzel sticks. Fill in the windowpanes with dark yellow icing. "Glue" graham sticks upside down to make the porch.

8 To make a pine tree, "glue" a sugar cone upside down next to the cabin. Cut spearmint leaves into two layers and stick the layers in rows on the cone. Repeat to make a second pine tree.

DUTCH WINDMILL

⅓ batch white
   royal icing

⅓ batch dark brown
   royal icing

⅓ batch green
   royal icing

Graham crackers
   (see diagram)

Small waffle cone,
   such as Keebler

4 chocolate sugar
   wafer cookies

Decorations

- gumdrops
- green sour straws
- spearmint leaves

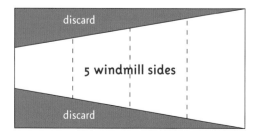

discard

5 windmill sides

discard

1 Using white icing, make the bottom of the windmill by "gluing" the five graham crackers together in a tower. The wide edges should be at the bottom and the narrow edges should meet at the top. "Glue" the waffle bowl upside down over the top.

2 Gently separate the top layer from each wafer cookie. Throw away the bottom layers that have the frosting on them. Cover the windmill in brown icing, then stick the wafer cookie tops to the windmill top to make the arms of the windmill. Using white icing, draw an X to connect the wafers.

3 Draw windows using white icing. Make tulips by cutting gumdrops in half and sticking each half upside down onto a piece of sour straw. Use pieces of gumdrops instead of icing to "glue" the tulips together. Spread green icing around the windmill to make the meadow. Stick the tulips into the green icing.

TIKI HUT

1/2 batch brown
   royal icing

1/2 batch royal icing
   divided into hot pink,
   turquoise, yellow,
   purple, and green

Graham crackers (see
   diagrams next page)

Shredded Wheat

Decorations
- pretzel sticks
- pretzel rods
- Andes Mints
- spearmint leaves
- orange gumdrops
- vanilla wafer
  cookies

1 To make the front and back of the hut, use brown icing to "glue" a horizontal point graham cracker to a whole graham cracker along the long edges. "Glue" a quarter cracker across the seam to help the two pieces stay together. Repeat with the second triangle piece and another whole cracker.

2 To make the roof pieces, cut a whole cracker in half diagonally to make two long triangles. "Glue" a triangle to a whole cracker along the long edges. "Glue" a quarter cracker across the seam. Repeat to make a second roof piece.

3 Put together the hut using the front and back pieces and two half crackers for the sides. "Glue" the roof pieces on top, so that the shortest edge of the roof is at the bottom and the long pointed edges meet at the top.

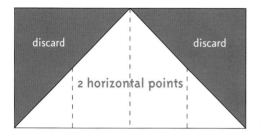

discard | 2 horizontal points | discard

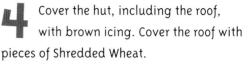

5 whole crackers

2 half crackers

4 quarter crackers

4 Cover the hut, including the roof, with brown icing. Cover the roof with pieces of Shredded Wheat.

5 Glue two Andes Mints horizontally to the front of the hut to make the door opening.

6 Using the different colors of icing, draw a door frame and designs on the front of the hut. Draw a tiki mask on either side of the door frame.

7 Make palm trees by "gluing" pretzel rods topped with pieces of spearmint leaves and position them next to the hut. Make bamboo torches using pretzel sticks with pieces of orange gumdrops stuck to the tops for the flames. Stick the torches into spearmint leaves and place them in front of the hut.

8 Crush the vanilla wafer cookies in a food processor to make sand. Spread the sand around the hut, making sure to cover the bottoms of the torches.

BIG RED BARN

$\frac{1}{4}$ batch white royal icing

$\frac{1}{4}$ batch red royal icing

$\frac{1}{4}$ batch brown royal icing

$\frac{1}{4}$ batch green royal icing

Graham crackers (see diagrams next page)

Decorations
• black licorice drops
• pretzel sticks
• yellow chocolate-covered sunflower seeds
• green sour straws
• brown M&Ms
• green gumdrops

1 To make the front of the barn, use white icing to "glue" two graham crackers together on the long sides. "Glue" a quarter cracker across the seam to help the two pieces stay together. "Glue" one of the barn top graham crackers to the top. Then "glue" a quarter cracker across the seam. Repeat to make the back of the barn.

2 To make one side of the barn, "glue" two whole crackers together along the long edges. "Glue" a quarter cracker across the seam. Repeat to make the second side.

3 Put together the barn using the front and back pieces and the sides. "Glue" two whole crackers against the top slanted edges of the barn top pieces. "Glue" the two remaining whole crackers to the open slanted edges to complete the roof.

4 Cover the barn with red icing. Save a little red icing for use in step 6. Draw doors on the barn front using white icing.

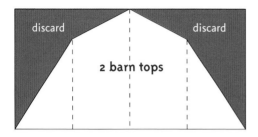

discard   discard

2 barn tops

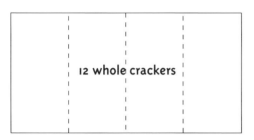

12 whole crackers

6 quarter crackers

Cover the roof with brown icing. Spread the green icing around the barn for grass.

5 Make a sheep by sticking four pretzel sticks into four licorice drops. Break off the bottoms of the sticks until you have the desired height of the sheep. "Glue" the four drops together. To make the head, stick a pretzel stick into another licorice drop and stick this into the sheep. Cut pieces of drops for the ears and stick them to the head. Pipe dots of white icing onto the sheep's body for fleece. Repeat to make a second sheep.

6 Make a sunflower by "gluing" chocolate-covered sunflower seeds to the back of a brown M&M. Cut a sour straw in half lengthwise and "glue" it to the back of the sunflower. Repeat to make as many sunflowers as desired. Let dry overnight, then "glue" the sunflowers to the barn using leftover red icing. Make leaves from green gumdrops and stick to the sunflower stems.

CARIBBEAN BUNGALOW

²/₃ batch white
   royal icing

¹/₃ batch yellow
   royal icing

Graham crackers (see
   diagrams next page)

Pretzel sticks

9 pretzel bites

Small waffle bowl,
   such as Keebler

Shredded Wheat

Decorations
- Andes Mints
- Fruit Stripe Gum
- pretzel rods
- spearmint leaves
- vanilla wafer
  cookies
- blue decorating
  sugar

1 To make the platform, use white icing to "glue" two whole graham crackers together along the long edges. "Glue" two more whole crackers on top in the opposite direction. You should have a square platform with two graham cracker layers.

2 "Glue" nine pretzel bites to the platform in a grid. These are the feet at the base of the platform. Gently turn the platform over and "glue" it to a cardboard base.

3 Cover the top and sides of the platform with white icing and pretzel sticks.

4 Make the bungalow on top of the platform using four half crackers. "Glue" the waffle bowl upside down on top of the bungalow.

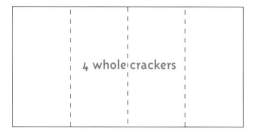

4 whole crackers

4 half crackers

5 Cover the bungalow in yellow icing. "Glue" pieces of Shredded Wheat to the roof.

6 Make windows and a door using Andes Mints and white icing. Use Fruit Stripe Gum for the shutters. Spread blue decorating sugar underneath and around the platform. Make palm trees using pretzel rods and spearmint leaves. Stick the ends of the trees into more spearmint leaves and stick them to the cardboard base. Crush vanilla wafers in a food processor to make sand. Spread the sand around the palm trees to make the beach.

FIREHOUSE

3/4 batch white royal icing, with about 1/2 cup tinted red

1/4 batch dark brown royal icing

Graham crackers (see diagrams next page)

Decorations

- Twizzlers Cherry Nibs
- Andes Mints
- mini Oreos
- cinnamon drops

1 To make the front of the firehouse, cut a whole cracker in half diagonally to make two long triangles. "Glue" the triangles together along the short edges. "Glue" a quarter cracker across the seam. "Glue" the short edges of three whole crackers along the bottom of this piece. "Glue" a quarter cracker across each seam. Repeat to make the back of the house.

2 To make one side of the firehouse, "glue" two whole crackers together along the long edges. "Glue" a quarter cracker across the seam. Repeat to make the second side.

3 "Glue" the front, back, and sides together to make the house.

4 To make the roof, "glue" two whole crackers together along the long edges. "Glue" a quarter cracker across the seam. Repeat to make the second roof piece. Carefully "glue" the roof pieces to the top of the house.

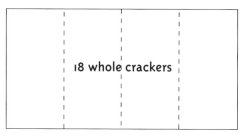

18 whole crackers

16 quarter crackers

5 Cover the roof with dark brown icing. Put bricks on the sides and back of the house by covering a portion of the wall with white icing, then arranging rows of Nibs to look like bricks. Keep going, doing small portions at a time, until the back and sides are covered.

6 To make the front, place bricks on the sides and top of the wall, leaving the middle uncovered. Cover the middle with white icing, then make garage door windows using four Andes Mints. Make a brick border around the garage door.

7 To make the fire engine, cut two whole crackers in half lengthwise to make four long skinny pieces. Cut one piece widthwise into three equal pieces. Make the truck using a long skinny piece for the bottom and a long skinny piece for each side. Use two little pieces for the ends. (Discard the third little piece.) "Glue" a stack of three Andes Mints across the top at the front end of the truck, about $1/2$ inch from the front edge. Lean an Andes Mint against the front side of the stack. Cover the entire truck in red icing. Draw details using white icing. Make wheels using mini Oreos and cinnamon drops.

THE OLD WOMAN WHO LIVED IN A SHOE

²/₃ batch purple
   royal icing

¹/₃ batch green
   royal icing

13 (2³/₄-inch) soft
   bakery cookies

Graham crackers
   (see diagram)

Decorations

• green licorice
  snaps
• yellow Chiclets
• rainbow Airheads
  Xtremes
• green sour straws
• gumdrops

1 Using the purple icing, "glue" eight cookies together in a stack. This will make the main part of the shoe. Cut the remaining cookies in half. "Glue" six cookie halves together in a stack. Turn the stack flat side down and place it against the stack of whole cookies. "Glue" three cookie halves together in a stack. Place this little stack at the end of the sideways stack to make the toe of the boot.

2 To make the roof, cut a half cracker in half diagonally to make two triangle pieces. "Glue" one triangle piece upright on top of the whole-cookie stack, at the back. "Glue" the second triangle on top at the front of the stack. "Glue" a half cracker on each side to make the roof.

3 Frost the entire shoe, except the roof, with purple icing. "Glue" green licorice snaps to the roof using green icing. Use green icing to make shoelaces.

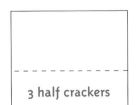

3 half crackers

4 Make the windows using yellow Chiclets for the windowpanes and Airheads Xtremes for the shutters. Make grass from green sour straws cut into small pieces. Use bits of gumdrops to stick the grass to the shoe. Make mushrooms from pieces of red and white gumdrops.

SWISS CHALET

3/4 batch brown
   royal icing

1/4 batch white
   royal icing

Graham crackers (see
   diagrams next page)

Decorations

- green gum
- flower confetti
- heart confetti
- Tootsie Rolls
- Smarties

1 To make the front of the house, use brown icing to "glue" two whole crackers together along the long edges. "Glue" a quarter cracker across the seam. "Glue" a horizontal point graham cracker along the top of the top cracker. Then "glue" a quarter cracker across the seam.

2 Repeat step 1 to make the back of the house.

3 To make one side of the house, "glue" two three-quarters crackers together along the long edges. "Glue" a quarter cracker across the seam. Repeat to make the second side of the house.

4 Put the house together using the front, back, and side pieces. "Glue" two whole crackers on each side for the roof.

5 Cover the entire house and roof with brown icing.

8 whole crackers

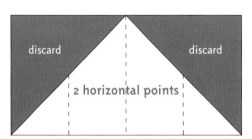

discard   discard

2 horizontal points

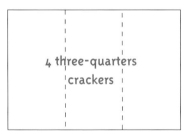

4 three-quarters crackers

6 quarter crackers

6 "Glue" white Smarties in a row underneath the roof eaves. Pipe brown icing along the top of the Smarties. Draw windows using white icing. Make shutters using green gum and white flower confetti. Make window boxes using Tootsie Rolls cut in half. "Glue" green flower confetti and red heart confetti to the window boxes. Draw designs using white icing.

BLUE DOLLHOUSE

1/3 batch white
   royal icing

1/3 batch light blue
   royal icing

1/3 batch green
   royal icing

Graham crackers (see
   diagrams next page)

Decorations
- white Smarties
- candy sticks
- spearmint leaves
- flower confetti
- orange licorice
  snaps

1 To make the front of the house, use white icing to "glue" two whole crackers together along the long edges. "Glue" a quarter cracker across the seam to help the pieces stay together. Repeat to make the back of the house.

2 To make one side of the house, "glue" a half cracker to the bottom of a vertical point piece. "Glue" a quarter cracker across the seam to help the two pieces stay together. Repeat to make the second side.

3 "Glue" the front, back, and sides together to make the house. "Glue" a whole cracker on each side for the roof.

4 To make the gable, cut two half crackers in half diagonally to make four triangle pieces. Throw away the fourth triangle. Pipe icing along the bottom side of one triangle and hold it gently at the bottom front of the roof. Still holding the triangle,

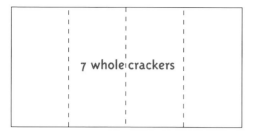

7 whole crackers

4 half crackers

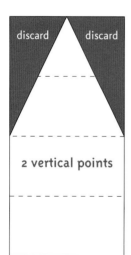

discard   discard

2 vertical points

4 quarter crackers

pipe icing along the top two sides of the triangle. "Glue" a triangle perpendicular to each side of the first triangle. The opposite edges of the second and third triangles should meet at the top. Pipe icing along this top seam and along the bottom edges of the second and third triangles, where they meet the roof.

5 Frost the whole house, except the roof, in blue icing. Make windows using pieces of Andes Mints and white icing. Draw a door using white icing.

6 To make the porch, cut a whole cracker in half lengthwise to make two long skinny pieces. "Glue" one piece along the bottom of the house. Cover the porch in white icing. Break the candy sticks into pieces about 2¹/₂ inches long. "Glue" two sticks on either end of the porch for pillars. "Glue" the second long skinny graham cracker piece to the house so that it rests on top of the candy sticks. Lift up the porch roof gently and "glue" two more candy sticks to the porch.

7 Decorate the roof and porch roof using white icing and white Smarties. Make a brick path using pieces of orange licorice snaps and white icing. Make flower bushes using pieces of spearmint leaves and flower confetti. Spread green icing around the house to make the yard.

MUSHROOM GNOME HOME

8 (3-inch) cookies

1 small waffle bowl, such as Keebler

1/2 batch off-white royal icing

1/4 batch red royal icing

1/4 batch brown royal icing

Necco Wafers

Tootsie Rolls

Decorations

- pretzel sticks
- Tootsie Rolls
- heart confetti
- flower confetti
- chocolate pebbles
- green sour straws
- speckled jelly beans

1 Using off-white icing, "glue" the 3-inch cookies together in a stack. "Glue" the waffle bowl upside down on top of the stack.

2 Cover the top of the mushroom with red icing. Place white Necco Wafers on top to make spots.

3 Cover the mushroom stem with off-white icing. Using brown icing, draw a door on the front. Place a Necco wafer on each side of the door for windows. Pipe thin lines of brown icing on the wafers to create window frames.

4 Shape a Tootsie Roll into a chimney and "glue" it at the back of the roof.

5 Make the mailbox using a pretzel stick stuck into a Tootsie Roll and a red heart confetti for the flag. Use chocolate pebbles for rocks, flower confetti for flowers, and sour straws cut into small pieces for grass. Use speckled jelly beans for the cobblestone path.

IGLOO

1 batch white royal icing

Sugar cubes

Decorations
- white gumdrops
- orange gumdrops
- black jelly beans
- Twizzlers black
  licorice Nibs
- blue decorating
  sugar

1 To make the first layer of the igloo, use icing to "glue" twenty-two sugar cubes in a circle. Building upwards, make more layers using fewer sugar cubes each time until you just have one cube at the top. As you make the layers, "glue" down the cubes with icing and spread the cubes out evenly along the layer beneath.

2 Make the entrance to the igloo using three layers of two cubes on each side. Cover the top with lots of icing. Fill in the gaps between all the cubes with icing.

3 Make the penguins by cutting the tops and sides off white gumdrops to reveal the sticky inside. Make wings from pieces of licorice Nibs and heads from black jelly beans cut in half. Make feet and beaks using pieces of orange gumdrops.

4 Spread white icing around the igloo and arrange the penguins in the icing. Sprinkle blue decorating sugar on one side of the igloo to make the ocean.

SEVEN DWARFS' COTTAGE

³/₄ batch off-white
   royal icing
¹/₄ batch dark brown
   royal icing
Graham crackers (see
   diagrams next page)
Corn Chex cereal

Decorations
- Andes Mints
- Tootsie Rolls
- pretzel sticks
- Twizzlers black
  licorice Nibs
- flower or heart
  confetti
- rock candy

1 To make the right half of the house, make the Easy Candy Cottage as directed on page 13. To make the front door piece, cut a half cracker in half diagonally to make two triangle pieces. "Glue" a triangle to a half cracker. "Glue" a quarter cracker across the seam. Set aside.

2 "Glue" a quarter cracker perpendicular to the front of the house, a fourth of the way in from the right side. Then "glue" another quarter cracker perpendicular to the front of the house, a fourth of the way in from the left side. "Glue" the second triangle across the two quarter pieces where the quarter pieces meet the roof. "Glue" the triangle-topped piece that you had set aside to the open ends of the two quarter crackers. "Glue" the last two quarter crackers on top of the structure to make a roof.

3 Cover the house with off-white icing. Draw a door shape on the front of the house using dark brown icing.

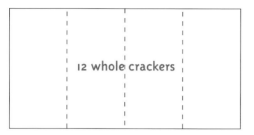

12 whole crackers

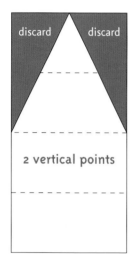

discard   discard

2 vertical points

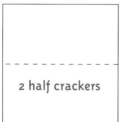

2 half crackers

4 Shape two Tootsie Rolls into tree trunks. "Glue" a quarter cracker above the door and use the tree trunks to hold up the porch roof.

5 To make the front of the left half of the house, cut a whole cracker in half diagonally to make two long skinny triangles. "Glue" the triangles together along the long straight edges. "Glue" a quarter cracker across the seam. "Glue" this piece to the long edge of a whole cracker. Then "glue" two quarter crackers across the seam.

6 Repeat step 5 to make the back of the house.

7 Build the left half of the house using the front and back pieces and one horizontal three-quarters cracker for each side. "Glue" two whole crackers on each side for the roof.

8 Cover the left half of the house with off-white icing. "Glue" Corn Chex onto both roofs for shingles. Use brown icing to draw the woodwork. Use Andes Mints for the windows and Tootsie Rolls for the shutters. "Glue" white confetti onto the shutters. Make pickaxes by cutting crescent shapes from Nibs and sticking them to pretzel sticks. Decorate yard with rock candy for jewels.

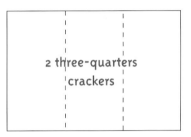

12 quarter crackers

2 three-quarters crackers

HAUNTED MANSION

$^1/_3$ batch white royal
icing, with about
$^1/_2$ cup tinted black

$^1/_3$ batch dark purple
royal icing

$^1/_3$ batch orange
royal icing

Graham crackers (see
diagrams next page)

. . . .

Decorations
- purple Chiclets
- orange Chiclets
- purple fruit slices
- yellow Chiclets
- black licorice
  twists
- orange M&Ms
- pumpkin candies
- gummy spiders

. . . .

1 To make the right "tower" of the house, cut a half cracker in half diagonally to make two triangles. Using white icing, "glue" a triangle to the short edge of a whole cracker. "Glue" a quarter cracker across the seam to help the two pieces stay together. Repeat to make a second triangle-topped piece. Make the tower using the triangle-topped pieces for the sides and one vertical whole cracker each for the front and the back. "Glue" two half crackers to the slanted eaves to make the roof.

2 Repeat step 1 to make the left tower.

3 To make the center tower, "glue" a half cracker to a whole cracker along the short edges. "Glue" a quarter cracker across the seam. Repeat three times to make four long pieces. "Glue" the four long pieces together to make the tower.

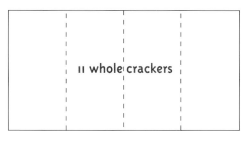

11 whole crackers

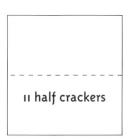

11 half crackers

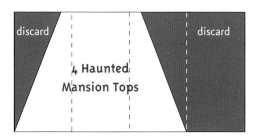

discard

4 Haunted Mansion Tops

discard

11 quarter crackers

4 "Glue" the four Haunted Mansion Top graham crackers together along the slanted lines to make a pyramid shape with a flat top. Then "glue" the last half cracker on top of the flat pyramid. "Glue" the flat pyramid on top of the center tower.

5 "Glue" a shorter tower to each side of the tall tower, about halfway back so that the tall tower sticks out in front of the two side towers.

6 Next cut about $1/2$ inch off the ends of three quarter graham crackers. Make a porch by stacking two of these crackers at the base of the front tower. Set aside the remaining cracker to make the porch roof later.

7 Frost the entire house, except the roof, in purple icing. While the icing is still wet, make windowpanes out of purple Chiclets and purple fruit slices and make shutters out of orange Chiclets. Use orange Chiclets for the front door.

8 Cut two pieces of black licorice to about $2^1/_2$ inches each. Frost the cut quarter cracker you set aside earlier with purple icing. Attach the porch roof above the door and prop it up using the black licorice pieces.

9 Frost the entire roof orange, then cover it with orange M&Ms. Make the roof railing by cutting black licorice into small pieces and some long strips and sticking them into the icing.

10 "Glue" yellow Chiclets to the center front of the roof. Pipe window frames onto all the windows using black icing.

11 "Glue" pumpkins and gummy spiders around the house.

SANTA'S CASTLE

¹/₂ batch off-white
   royal icing

¹/₄ batch red icing

¹/₄ batch green icing

Graham crackers (see
   diagrams next page)

16 vanilla sandwich
   cookies

2 sugar cones

Decorations
- apple gummy ring
- Fruit Stripe Gum
- yellow Chiclets
- yellow fruit slices
- Sour Skittles
- spearmint leaves
- waffle cone
- peppermints
- Big Red gum
- cinnamon candies

1 To make the front of the castle, use off-white icing to "glue" three whole crackers together along the long edges. "Glue" a quarter cracker across each seam to help the pieces stay together. Repeat with three more whole crackers and two quarter crackers to make the back of the castle.

2 To make the sides of the castle, cut a half cracker in half diagonally to make two triangle pieces. To make one side, "glue" a triangle to a whole cracker along the short edge. "Glue" a quarter cracker across the seam. Repeat to make the second side.

3 "Glue" the front, back, and sides together to make the castle.

4 To make the roof, "glue" a half cracker to a whole cracker along the short edge. "Glue" a quarter cracker across the seam. Repeat to make the other side of the roof. Pipe icing along the slanted rooflines. Carefully place the long roof pieces on top of the slanted rooflines.

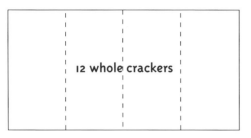

12 whole crackers

11 quarter crackers

4 half crackers

5 To make the front part of the house, cut a half cracker in half diagonally to make two triangle pieces. "Glue" a triangle to a whole cracker along the short edge. "Glue" a quarter cracker across the seam. Cut a whole cracker in half lengthwise to make two long skinny pieces. "Glue" each long piece perpendicular to the front of the house, one-third of the way in from the left side and one-third of the way in from the right side. "Glue" the triangle-topped whole cracker to the long skinny crackers. "Glue" the second triangle piece at the top back of the long skinny pieces. Pipe icing along the slanted lines. "Glue" a quarter cracker on each side to make the little roof.

6 To make a tower, stack eight sandwich cookies, placing icing between each cookie. "Glue" a sugar cone to the top. Repeat to make a second tower. Place a tower on each side of the castle.

7 Frost the castle off-white. Frost the roof and tower tops red. Make windows using yellow Chiclets, yellow fruit slices, red icing, and green sour straws. Make the front door using two pieces of red Fruit Stripe gum, cutting the top corners into a rounded shape. Add a cinnamon candy for a doorknob and an apple gummy ring for a wreath. Make garlands across the rooflines using green icing.

8 Make bushes using spearmint leaves. Make a tree using an upside-down waffle cone and thin layers of spearmint leaves. "Glue" Sour Skittles to the tree for ornaments. Make a path in front of the house using peppermints. Make a North Pole sign using a peppermint candy stick and a piece of Big Red gum wrapped around the top. Write "North Pole" on the gum using white icing.

DRACULA'S CASTLE

3/4 batch dark gray
royal icing

1/4 batch black
royal icing

A few tablespoons
yellow royal icing

Graham crackers (see
diagrams next page)

1 package vanilla
wafer cookies

12 sandwich cookies

2 sugar cones

1 waffle cone

5 flat-bottom waffle
bowls, such as
Joy or Kroger

Decorations

• black licorice
twists and Nibs

• yellow Chiclets

• Tootsie Rolls

1 Make the hill by using royal icing to "glue" four waffle bowls upside down in a square onto your cardboard base. "Glue" a whole cracker across the front and back bowls on the right side of the square and another whole cracker across the front and back bowls on the left side. Then "glue" a whole cracker across the two front bowls, on top of the other two crackers, and a whole cracker across the two back bowls. "Glue" a third cracker between the two front and back crackers. You should now have three whole crackers lying on top of two whole crackers.

2 To make the front of the short rectangle tower, "glue" a half cracker to the bottom of a vertical point cracker. "Glue" a quarter cracker across the seam to help the pieces stay together. Repeat to make the back of the tower. Build the tower at the front of the hill, using the front and back pieces you have just made and two whole crackers for the side pieces. Make the roof using two half crackers.

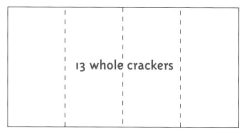

13 whole crackers

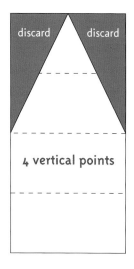

discard   discard

4 vertical points

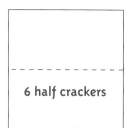

6 half crackers

6 quarter crackers

3 To make the front of the tall back tower, "glue" the short side of a whole cracker to the bottom of a point cracker. "Glue" a quarter cracker across the seam. Repeat to make the back of the tower. Make each side by "gluing" two whole crackers together along the short edges. "Glue" a quarter cracker across the seam. Build the tower at the back left of the hill, using the front and back pieces and the side pieces you have just made. Make the roof using two half crackers.

4 Make the left round tower by "gluing" seven vanilla wafers together in a stack, then "gluing" a sugar cone upside down on top of the stack. Repeat to make the right round tower, only this time using nine vanilla wafers. Repeat to make the back round tower, this time using twelve sandwich cookies and a waffle cone.

5 Create the path by making five stacks of vanilla wafers, using six wafers for one stack, five for the next, then four, then three, then two. Arrange the stacks from tallest to shortest to make a path.

6 Cover the towers, hill, and path with dark gray icing. Cover the tower roofs with black icing.

7 Make the moon from a waffle bowl by gently breaking off the sides of the bowl so that the bottom circle remains. Cover the circle with yellow icing and stick it to the back of the tall left tower.

8 Cut bat shapes from black licorice twists and place on the moon. Make the front door using Tootsie Rolls and Nibs, and draw a circle on the front with black icing.

9 Make windows using Chiclets. Make trees by cutting the top half of licorice twists into strips and bending them outward. "Glue" the trees to the towers and the sides of the path.

SILLY POLKA-DOT HOUSE

½ batch green
   royal icing

¼ batch blue royal icing

¼ batch purple
   royal icing

Graham crackers
   (see diagrams)

Decorations
- M&Ms
- Spree candies

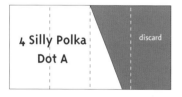

4 Silly Polka Dot A   discard

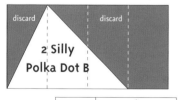

2 Silly Polka Dot B   discard   discard

5 half crackers

3 three-quarters crackers

1 Using green icing, make the first floor of the house with two Silly Polka Dot A crackers for the front and back of the house and two half crackers for the sides. Make sure the straight side of the front and back pieces is on the right and the slanted side is on the left. "Glue" a three-quarters cracker across the top.

2 Repeat step 1 to make the second floor, this time placing the straight side on the left and the slanted side on the right. "Glue" a three-quarters cracker across the top.

3 Make the top floor using the Silly Polka Dot B pieces as the front and back, making sure the longer side of the triangle is on the left. Make the roof using a half cracker for the short right side and a three-quarters cracker for the long left side.

4 Frost the entire house in green icing. Draw windows and a door using purple icing, then outline in blue. Outline the sides of the house in blue. Decorate using M&Ms and Spree candies.

PINK CASTLE IN THE CLOUDS

¹/₃ batch white
  royal icing

¹/₃ batch pink
  royal icing

¹/₃ batch purple
  royal icing

33 vanilla wafers

5 ice cream cups

5 waffle cones

Graham crackers (see
  diagrams next page)

Decorations
- purple jelly candy
- pink candy sticks
- pink gum
- pink cotton candy

1 To make one front tower, use white icing to "glue" five vanilla wafers together in a stack. "Glue" the bottom of an ice cream cup to the top of the cookie stack. Repeat to make the second front tower.

2 Breaking off small pieces at a time, gently remove about 1 inch from the top rim of a waffle cone. (This will help it fit better into the ice cream cup.) Using a serrated knife, gently saw about 1 inch off the bottom of the cone to make a hole for the candy stick. Turn the waffle cone upside down and "glue" it into the top of one of the towers. Repeat for the second tower.

3 Repeat the first two steps to make the two back towers, except use seven vanilla wafers for each tower. Make the center tower in the same way, except use nine vanilla wafers. Be careful with the towers—they can easily fall down until they're stabilized.

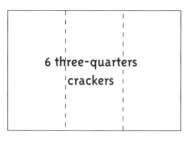

6 three-quarters crackers

2 quarter crackers

4 To make the front of the castle, "glue" two three-quarters crackers together along the long sides. "Glue" a quarter cracker across the seam to help the two pieces stay together. "Glue" the two shortest towers to either side of the graham cracker wall.

5 Make each side of the castle by "gluing" a three-quarters cracker vertically between a short front tower and a medium back tower.

6 Make the back of the castle by "gluing" the remaining two three-quarters crackers together along the long sides. "Glue" a quarter cracker across the seam. "Glue" this wall between the two back towers.

7 Place the tallest tower inside the castle and "glue" it against the back wall.

8 Cut brick shapes from purple jelly candy. Frost the entire castle except the waffle cones in pink icing. While the icing is still wet, stick the "bricks" to the towers and walls. Draw a castle gate using purple icing.

9 Frost the waffle cones with purple icing, then put a candy stick inside each waffle cone hole. Cut flag shapes out of pink gum and "glue" them to the top of each candy stick.

10 Spread cotton candy around the base of the castle for clouds.

Also Available

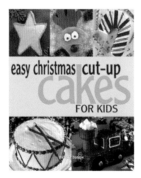